Debating
Challenge!

Developing
Major
Debate Skills

Neill Porteous

3

Table of **Contents**

Features

The Debating Challenge series help English learners to develop key debating skills.

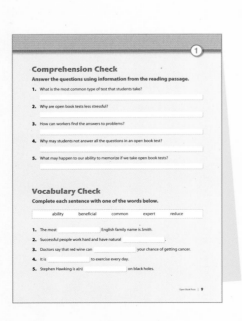

Introduction and Warm-Up Questions

● A variety of activities that introduce each unit's theme to students

● Warm-up questions that allow students to understand major aspects of each unit's theme

Reading

● Carefully chosen debating issues that are relevant to today's teenagers

● Expertly written texts that present different opinions clearly and logically

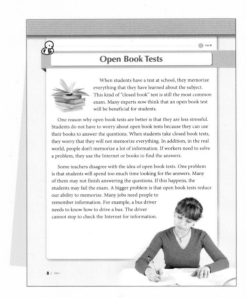

Comprehension Check & Vocabulary Check

● Comprehension questions that help students understand each unit's text

● Vocabulary questions that enable students to learn how to use key words in context

Opinion Practice

- Two different activities that teach learners how to support and refute different opinions

- Various opinions that address major aspects of each unit's debating issue

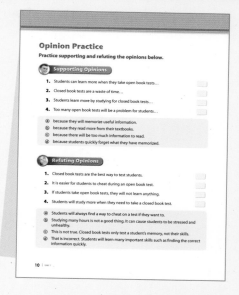

Opinion Examples

- Two different opinions that are based on logical reasoning

- Text analysis activities that reinforce critical reading and thinking skills

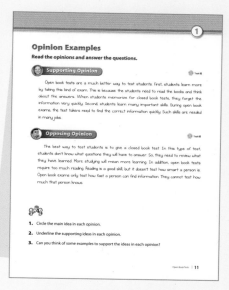

Discussion Questions & Let's Debate

- Discussion questions that are closely associated with each unit's debating issue

- Let's Debate section that invites students to explore and debate major issues

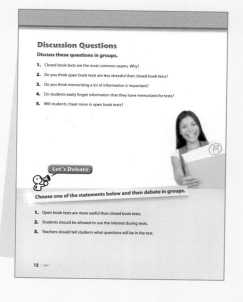

Unit 1
Open Book Tests

Students take hundreds of tests at school. Most students dislike tests because they need to memorize a lot of information. Then, will it be a better idea if students take open book tests?

There is a test for almost every subject that we study. Think about the subjects you study at school. Which classes have the easiest or most difficult exams? Make sure you explain your reasons.

	Best Tests	Reasons
1.		
2.		

	Worst Tests	Reasons
1.		
2.		

Warm-Up Questions

1. Why do schools give tests?

2. What do you think about tests?

3. What is the hardest thing about taking a test?

Open Book Tests

When students have a test at school, they memorize everything that they have learned about the subject. This kind of "closed book" test is still the most common exam. Many experts now think that an open book test will be beneficial for students.

One reason why open book tests are better is that they are less stressful. Students do not have to worry about open book tests because they can use their books to answer the questions. When students take closed book tests, they worry that they will not memorize everything. In addition, in the real world, people don't memorize a lot of information. If workers need to solve a problem, they use the Internet or books to find the answers.

Some teachers disagree with the idea of open book tests. One problem is that students will spend too much time looking for the answers. Many of them may not finish answering the questions. If this happens, the students may fail the exam. A bigger problem is that open book tests reduce our ability to memorize. Many jobs need people to remember information. For example, a bus driver needs to know how to drive a bus. The driver cannot stop to check the Internet for information.

Comprehension Check

Answer the questions using information from the reading passage.

1. What is the most common type of test that students take?

2. Why are open book tests less stressful?

3. How can workers find the answers to problems?

4. Why may students not answer all the questions in an open book test?

5. What may happen to our ability to memorize if we take open book tests?

Vocabulary Check

Complete each sentence with one of the words below.

ability	beneficial	common	expert	reduce

1. The most _____ English family name is *Smith*.

2. Successful people work hard and have natural _____.

3. Doctors say that red wine can _____ your chance of getting cancer.

4. It is _____ to exercise every day.

5. Stephen Hawking is a(n) _____ on black holes.

Opinion Practice

Practice supporting and refuting the opinions below.

 Supporting Opinions

1. Students can learn more when they take open book tests…

2. Closed book tests are a waste of time…

3. Students learn more by studying for closed book tests…

4. Too many open book tests will be a problem for students…

   ⓐ because they will memorize useful information.

   ⓑ because they read more from their textbooks.

   ⓒ because there will be too much information to read.

   ⓓ because students quickly forget what they have memorized.

Refuting Opinions

1. Closed book tests are the best way to test students.

2. It is easier for students to cheat during an open book test.

3. If students take open book tests, they will not learn anything.

4. Students will study more when they need to take a closed book test.

   ⓐ Students will always find a way to cheat on a test if they want to.

   ⓑ Studying many hours is not a good thing. It can cause students to be stressed and unhealthy.

   ⓒ This is not true. Closed book tests only test a student's memory, not their skills.

   ⓓ That is incorrect. Students will learn many important skills such as finding the correct information quickly.

Opinion Examples

Read the opinions and answer the questions.

 Supporting Opinion

 **02** / Unit 1

Open book tests are a much better way to test students. First, students learn more by taking this kind of exam. This is because the students need to read the books and think about the answers. When students memorize for closed book tests, they forget the information very quickly. Second, students learn many important skills. During open book exams, the test takers need to find the correct information quickly. Such skills are needed in many jobs.

 Opposing Opinion

 **03** / Unit 1

The best way to test students is to give a closed book test. In this type of test, students don't know what questions they will have to answer. So, they need to review what they have learned. More studying will mean more learning. In addition, open book tests require too much reading. Reading is a good skill, but it doesn't test how smart a person is. Open book exams only test how fast a person can find information. They cannot test how much that person knows.

1. Circle the main idea in each opinion.

2. Underline the supporting ideas in each opinion.

3. Can you think of some examples to support the ideas in each opinion?

Discussion Questions

Discuss these questions in groups.

1. Closed book tests are the most common exams. Why?

2. Do you think open book tests are less stressful than closed book tests?

3. Do you think memorizing a lot of information is important?

4. Do students easily forget information that they have memorized for tests?

5. Will students cheat more in open book tests?

Choose one of the statements below and then debate in groups.

1. Open book tests are more useful than closed book tests.

2. Students should be allowed to use the Internet during tests.

3. Teachers should tell students what questions will be in the test.

Unit 2
Choosing Where to Shop

When it is time to buy food, we have a choice. We can go to small markets near our homes. Or we can go to a large supermarket. Which is the better choice?

Fill in the boxes below. Decide if you will buy the listed items in a small market or in a large supermarket. Explain your decisions to your classmates.

soft drinks	vegetables	milk	trash cans	a new TV set
coffee	bread	chewing gum	sushi	eggs

Small Market	**Large Supermarket**

Warm-Up Questions

1. Do you like to go food shopping?

2. Do you like to go to small markets or large supermarkets?

3. What is the worst day to go food shopping? Why?

Choosing Where to Shop

Everybody needs to buy their food each week. When it is time to go food shopping, does your family go to the local market or drive to a large supermarket? There are good and bad things about both types of markets. Which market is better?

Many people think that small markets are much better places to purchase the things that we need. One reason is that small markets are usually a short distance from our homes. Therefore, we can walk and buy the things that we need very easily. This is much faster than driving to a supermarket. Another great thing is that the foods are usually much fresher than those in supermarkets. This is important because fresh foods taste much better and are healthier.

Many shoppers believe that large supermarkets are great places to shop. Many supermarkets are huge. Because these stores are so big, they have a wide variety of products. This is great for customers because they can buy everything that they need at one time. Another benefit is that large supermarkets are open many hours each day. Sometimes they are open 24 hours a day. This is really convenient because customers can go shopping whenever they want.

Comprehension Check

Answer the questions using information from the reading passage.

1. How often do people need to buy their food?

2. Why is it good to live a short distance from a small market?

3. Why is it important to eat fresh foods?

4. What is the benefit of shopping at a huge supermarket?

5. Why can supermarket customers go shopping whenever they want?

Vocabulary Check

Complete each sentence with one of the words below.

fresh	huge	local	types	variety

1. The _____ police protect us from criminals.

2. My friend's dog is _____. It is as big as me.

3. There are many _____ of spiders in nature.

4. I have a _____ of hobbies. I never get bored.

5. I have bought bread that is very _____. It is still warm and soft.

Opinion Practice

Practice supporting and refuting the opinions below.

Supporting Opinions

1. It is easy to park our cars at supermarkets…

2. People in small markets know more about their products…

3. Small markets are usually cheaper…

4. It is interesting to shop at supermarkets…

ⓐ because we can see many products from all over the world.

ⓑ because the store owners give big discounts to customers.

ⓒ because the parking lots are so big.

ⓓ because they sell only several types of products.

Refuting Opinions

1. Supermarkets often have very big sales.

2. Foods in local markets are fresher.

3. We can get to know the workers in small markets.

4. It is very convenient to drive to supermarkets.

ⓐ I doubt this. Workers in small markets are usually very busy because they have many different things to do.

ⓑ I disagree. We can get stuck in traffic jams. Then, we need to wait to park our cars. It can take a long time.

ⓒ I disagree. Local markets cannot spend much money on technology to keep their foods really fresh.

ⓓ I doubt this. Most of the time, supermarket prices are the same as or higher than those of local markets.

Opinion Examples

Read the opinions and answer the questions.

 Supporting Opinion

 **05** / Unit 2

   Shopping in small markets is better than going to large supermarkets. One reason is that it is less stressful to go to local markets. We can walk there in a couple of minutes. When we go to the supermarket, we usually have to drive and then waste time looking for a parking space. Another great thing is that people in local markets know all about the products they sell. This is good for customers because they will know exactly where the food came from. They will also know that the food is safe.

 Opposing Opinion

 **06** / Unit 2

   When we need to go shopping, it is much better to go to a large supermarket. One of the great things is that supermarkets are interesting. We can buy foods and other products from all around the world. It is exciting to try different items. Another great thing is that supermarkets spend a lot of money to keep their foods really fresh. This is important because foods that are not fresh don't taste good, and they are bad for our health.

1. Circle the main idea in each opinion.

2. Underline the supporting ideas in each opinion.

3. Can you think of some examples to support the ideas in each opinion?

Discussion Questions

Discuss these questions in groups.

1. Do you think it is easy to go to a large supermarket? Why?

2. Do you like to know where the things you buy come from?

3. Is it important to have local stores and markets?

4. When we go food shopping, the price is the most important thing. Do you agree or disagree? Why?

5. Do you think foods in local markets are fresher than those in supermarkets?

 Let's Debate

Choose one of the statements below and then debate in groups.

1. It is better to shop in small markets and stores.

2. We should not buy foods from foreign countries.

3. Shopping in local markets is better for our environment.

No Electronic Devices During Break Time

Students cannot use electronic devices during class time. Some people say that students should not use such devices during break time either. What do you think?

Imagine it is now break time at school. What three things do you want to do during this time? Write your ideas and reasons in the table below. Explain your answers to your classmates.

	Activity	Reasons
1.		
2.		
3.		

Warm-Up Questions

1. What do you usually do during break time?

2. Is it important to be active or to relax during break time?

3. How will you feel if you cannot use an electronic device during break time?

No Electronic Devices During Break Time

When the bell rings for break time, students usually start using their electronic devices immediately. In other words, they begin using devices such as cellphones right away. They use those devices until the next lesson starts. Should schools stop the students from using them during recess?

Some people say that schools should stop students from using electronic devices during break time. One reason is that they are dangerous. During the break, students text and walk around at the same time. They don't look where they are going. This can cause accidents. Another reason is that students will talk to each other and be more active during break. In the past, students chatted and played many sports and games. These are much better things to do during break time.

Other people say that it is not a good idea to stop students from using electronic devices during break time. Recess is students' free time. If students are happy playing games or checking their messages, they should be allowed to do these things. In addition, students use these devices to

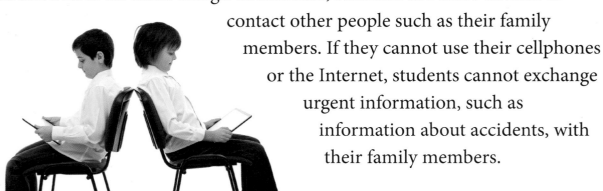

contact other people such as their family members. If they cannot use their cellphones or the Internet, students cannot exchange urgent information, such as information about accidents, with their family members.

Comprehension Check

Answer the questions using information from the reading passage.

1. What do students usually do when break time starts?

2. Why can electronic devices cause accidents?

3. What did students do during break time in the past?

4. Why should students be allowed to use their electronic devices during break time?

5. Why will it be a problem if students cannot use their electronic devices during break time?

Vocabulary Check

Complete each sentence with one of the words below.

| chat | exchange | immediately | recess | urgent |

1. I like _____ at my school because I can play with my classmates.

2. My friends and I like to go to the café and _____.

3. If we get soap in our eyes, we need to wash it away _____.

4. Excuse me. I have to make a(n) _____ phone call.

5. I like holidays because I can _____ gifts with my friends.

Opinion Practice

Practice supporting and refuting the opinions below.

 Supporting Opinions

1. Listening to music is good for students' learning…

2. If schools do not allow electronic devices, that will make students more active…

3. Using electronic devices during recess is not a waste of time…

4. Using electronic devices during recess is bad for students' health…

ⓐ because many students check the news, weather, or their schedule.

ⓑ because they feel tired and have sore fingers.

ⓒ because they are more motivated after listening to their favorite songs.

ⓓ because they will have nothing else to do.

 Refuting Opinions

1. Students will be more active if electronic devices are not allowed.

2. Using electronic devices helps students relax before their next lesson.

3. It is dangerous to walk around and use electronic devices.

4. Break time will be boring without cellphones, music players, or computer games.

ⓐ This is not true. Students will find fun things to do without using those devices.

ⓑ I disagree. Students get very excited when they play games or text their friends. They are not ready to study when break time finishes.

ⓒ I doubt it. They will just sit down and relax. Most students will probably sleep.

ⓓ I disagree. Most students sit down and use their devices during recess.

Opinion Examples

Read the opinions and answer the questions.

 Supporting Opinion

 **08** / Unit 3

Schools should stop students from using electronic devices during break time. One benefit is that students will be more active. Children will do more activities. If schools allow students to use electronic devices, they will sit in silence with their devices. Being more active can help reduce obesity. Another benefit is that students will be more ready to learn. If there are no electronic devices, students will not have sore eyes and fingers. Therefore, they can learn more in class.

 Opposing Opinion

 **09** / Unit 3

It is not a good idea for schools to stop students from using electronic devices during break time. These devices help students to relax. These days, students are really busy all the time and feel stressed. Being able to play a game, text a friend, or listen to a good song can help them relax. In addition, break time will be very boring without electronic devices. They are very important to us and make us happy. Using them is more exciting than playing boring games with our classmates.

1. Circle the main idea in each opinion.

2. Underline the supporting ideas in each opinion.

3. Can you think of some examples to support the ideas in each opinion?

Discussion Questions

Discuss these questions in groups.

1. Do you think electronic devices can cause accidents during recess?

2. Do students in your class talk to each other much during break time?

3. Should your school be allowed to tell you what to do during break time?

4. Do you think students use their electronic devices for important things during break time?

5. Will students be more active during recess if they cannot use electronic devices?

Let's Debate

Choose one of the statements below and then debate in groups.

1. Electronic devices should not be allowed during break time.

2. Students will be healthier if electronic devices are not allowed.

3. It is impossible for schools to stop students from using electronic devices during recess.

The Olympic Games Are a Waste of Money

Many countries really want to host the Olympics. As a result, they spend a lot of time and money. But it may be a waste of money to host the Olympic Games.

 **The Olympic Games have many different sports and different events. If you are allowed to choose only three sports events for the Olympics, which ones will you choose? Why?**

Sports Event 1:
Reason:
Sports Event 2:
Reason:
Sports Event 3:
Reason:

Warm-Up Questions

1. Do you like to watch the Olympics on television?

2. Are you happy that your country wants to host the Olympics?

3. Do you want to watch the Olympics live at a stadium?

MP3
DC3-04

The Olympic Games Are a Waste of Money

The Olympic Games are the biggest sports event in the world. Athletes from around 200 countries come together to win a gold medal. Finding out who is the best athlete is great, but the Olympics are so expensive. Should countries spend so much money?

Some people argue that hosting the Olympics is a waste of money. One reason is that the host country needs to spend a lot of money to build very expensive stadiums and buildings. This money can be used to improve the health and education of the population. Another reason is that these stadiums and other facilities are not needed after the Games have finished. As a result, they still cost a lot of money although they stay empty. This is not good for the host country.

Other people argue that the Olympics are not a waste of money. In fact, it is a great idea to spend money on the Olympic Games. First, people will feel very happy. They will see the best athletes in the world and have a good time. Second, many children and adults will feel inspired by having the Olympics in their country. As a result, many people will begin to play sports. People who play sports are much healthier.

Comprehension Check

Answer the questions using information from the reading passage.

1. How many countries take part in the Olympics?

2. Why do host countries need to spend a lot of money?

3. What happens to the stadiums and other facilities after the Olympics have finished?

4. People will be happy that their country will host the Olympics. Why?

5. Why will many people start playing sports after watching the Olympics?

Vocabulary Check

Complete each sentence with one of the words below.

education	empty	facilities	inspired	population

1. I felt _____ to start writing stories after meeting my favorite author.

2. A good _____ can help poor children to succeed.

3. A(n) _____ box does not have anything in it.

4. The _____ of South Korea is now more than 50 million people.

5. The _____ at the hotel were great. There was a swimming pool, an Internet café, and a movie theater.

Opinion Practice

Practice supporting and refuting the opinions below.

 Supporting Opinions

1. It is silly to spend so much money on the Olympics…

2. Hosting the Olympics is great for a country…

3. It will be better to spend money helping poor countries…

4. The Olympics can help improve cities and countries…

ⓐ because they cannot afford food, clothes, and shelter.

ⓑ because many tourists will visit and spend a lot of money.

ⓒ because they only last for two weeks.

ⓓ because they build many useful things, such as roads, subways, and parks.

 Refuting Opinions

1. The Olympics inspire people to play sports and exercise.

2. The Olympics can make a lot of profit.

3. If a country hosts the Olympics, it will be left with many useless stadiums.

4. The Olympics cost the government too much money.

ⓐ I disagree. The government also gets a lot of money back because of tax, and more people will have jobs. It is very good for the government.

ⓑ I don't think so. Not many people want to exercise after watching the Olympics.

ⓒ I disagree. Ordinary citizens can use those stadiums to exercise.

ⓓ I don't think so. The government loses a lot of money because of the Olympics.

Opinion Examples

Read the opinions and answer the questions.

 Supporting Opinion　　　　　 **11** / Unit 4

It is not a good idea to spend large amounts of money on the Olympics. That money can be used to help people in poor countries. Many of these people do not have enough food to eat or water to drink. We should think about others before building a stadium that no one will use. In addition, people don't improve their lifestyles after watching the Olympics. After a week or two, they forget about exercising and continue watching TV or playing computer games.

 Opposing Opinion　　　　　 **12** / Unit 4

Spending money on the Olympics can really help a country. The first reason is that the government will build many stadiums and other facilities for the Olympic Games. This helps to create a lot of jobs for ordinary people. If more people have jobs, the government can get more money. Another benefit is that many tourists from all over the world will come to watch the Olympics. They will spend a lot of money when they visit. This will also mean that there are more jobs for the host country's citizens.

1. Circle the main idea in each opinion.

2. Underline the supporting ideas in each opinion.

3. Can you think of some examples to support the ideas in each opinion?

Discussion Questions

Discuss these questions in groups.

1. Do you think it is good for a country to have many stadiums and sports facilities?

2. Do the Olympics inspire people to be more active and healthy? Why?

3. Is it more important for the government to improve its own country or help poor countries around the world?

4. Is it a good thing for many tourists to visit your country during the Olympics? Why?

5. Which building should the government construct: a hospital or a stadium?

Let's Debate

Choose one of the statements below and then debate in groups.

1. It is a waste of money to host the Olympics.

2. It is better to host the Summer Olympics than the Winter Olympics.

3. More people will visit a country that has hosted the Olympics.

Unit 5
Changing the School Calendar

These days, students go to school for two long semesters and have two long vacations each year. Many experts think this system is not helpful. They want schools to have shorter but more regular vacations.

Different people have different ideas about school semesters. Read the notice below and think about how students, parents, and teachers may feel. Make some notes in the table.

Notice:

The school year will change. From next March, students will have an eight-week semester and then they will have a two-week vacation. This schedule will be repeated all year.

The Principal

	Students	Teachers	Parents
Their Opinions			

Warm-Up Questions

1. Do you enjoy long school vacations?

2. What activities can students do during school vacations? Which activity do you want to do most?

3. How do you feel during the school semesters? Explain why you feel this way.

Changing the School Calendar

Each semester, students have to go to school for four or five months before they have a vacation. This can make them very tired. Experts say that it is a sensible idea to change the school schedule so that students can have vacations more frequently.

Some people argue that schools should have shorter semesters. One benefit is that students will not get so tired. As a result, students can study hard for a couple of months and then take a break. This will help prevent students from getting too tired. Another benefit is that shorter vacations will stop students from forgetting all the things that they learn during the semester. Teachers will not have to repeat the same lesson again. Instead, they can teach different lessons.

Other people argue that schools should not change their schedules. One problem is that shorter vacations will not be good for students. If the vacations are too short, students cannot do anything interesting or go far away. They will have less chance to learn new things during the 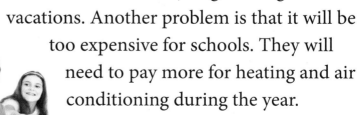 vacations. Another problem is that it will be too expensive for schools. They will need to pay more for heating and air conditioning during the year.

Comprehension Check

Answer the questions using information from the reading passage.

1. How long is each school semester?

2. Why will shorter semesters stop students from getting very tired?

3. If the vacations are shorter, teachers will not have to teach the same lesson again. Why?

4. Why will shorter vacations not be good for students?

5. Why will the new schedule be too expensive for schools?

Vocabulary Check

Complete each sentence with one of the words below.

frequently	prevent	repeat	semester	sensible

1. In the United States, a _____ usually lasts 18 weeks.

2. My brother exercises _____. As a result, he is healthy and strong.

3. My friends think that I am a _____ person because I don't do silly things.

4. Eating tomatoes can _____ people from getting cancer.

5. In some countries, students who fail need to _____ the same grade again.

Opinion Practice

Practice supporting and refuting the opinions below.

 Supporting Opinions

1. Students need longer vacations…

2. Many short school vacations are difficult for parents…

3. Shorter vacations are good for students…

4. Shorter vacations are less stressful for parents…

ⓐ because they don't have to spend much money at one time.

ⓑ because it takes a long time to stop feeling tired.

ⓒ because they need to keep organizing activities for their children.

ⓓ because they will not have time to get bored.

Refuting Opinions

1. Students will forget less during shorter vacations.

2. Students cannot do anything interesting when they have short vacations.

3. We need long vacations so that students and teachers can rest well.

4. Having more vacations means that students can do many interesting activities in the spring and fall.

ⓐ I disagree. There are so many interesting things that students can do in just one day.

ⓑ I don't think so. There are not many interesting activities that students can do in the spring and fall.

ⓒ I disagree. Students always forget the things they learn. They even forget what they learned the day before.

ⓓ This isn't true. People can feel great after just a few days' rest.

Opinion Examples

Read the opinions and answer the questions.

 Supporting Opinion

 **14** / Unit 5

It is a great idea to make the school semesters shorter and increase the number of vacations. One advantage is that students will not be bored during the vacations. During the longer summer and winter vacations, children have nothing to do. This will not happen with shorter breaks. Another advantage of having more vacations is that students can enjoy spring and fall. These are really great seasons to be on vacation. This is because the temperature is perfect to play outside.

 Opposing Opinion

 **15** / Unit 5

It is not a sensible idea to change the school schedule. The first reason is that students need a long break from school. The long winter and summer vacations are perfect for forgetting about school. They are perfect for doing something fun. The second reason is that many short vacations will be a problem for parents. They will have to keep organizing activities for their children. This will take a lot of time. Also, it may be expensive because the parents need to pay for more activities for their children.

1. Circle the main idea in each opinion.

2. Underline the supporting ideas in each opinion.

3. Can you think of some examples to support the ideas in each opinion?

Discussion Questions

Discuss these questions in groups.

1. Do you get bored during winter or summer vacations?

2. Do you want to have more school vacations during the year?

3. Do you think students will forget less if they have shorter vacations?

4. Do you think your parents want you to have two long school vacations? Or do they prefer more vacations that are shorter?

5. Is a two-week vacation long enough for students to rest?

Let's Debate

Choose one of the statements below and then debate in groups.

1. The school year should be changed so that semesters are shorter and students have more frequent vacations.

2. Teachers will be unhappy with many short vacations.

3. Short vacations are not fun.

Unit 6
Choosing the Class President

Most schools have class presidents. The class president's job is to lead the class and communicate with the teacher. How should we choose this person? Should the class vote or should the principal choose the president?

Imagine that you are the president of your class. What three changes will you make to the class to improve students' school experience?

	Change	Reasons
1.		
2.		
3.		

Warm-Up Questions

1. Is it important to have a class president?

2. Do you want to be class president?

3. Is it more important for a class president to be popular or to do a good job?

Choosing the Class President

Every year, many students try to become the presidents of their classes. The problem is that there can only be one winner. Usually, students vote for the person who they want to be class president. Will it be better if the school principal chooses each class president?

Some people argue that it is a great idea for the school principal to choose the class president. The first reason is that the principal will select the best student for the job. The principal will not choose the most popular student. He or she knows that a popular student does not always do a good job. The second reason is that the principal can select a student who can work well with the school staff. The class president, the principal, and the school staff should work together to make the school a better place.

Other people argue that students should choose the president of their class. This is because the students know each other best. They know who will be a good president during the school year. Another reason is that if students vote for the class president, they will listen to orders that the person gives. Nobody likes to obey a leader who they have not chosen.

Comprehension Check

Answer the questions using information from the reading passage.

1. Who usually choose the class president?

2. What kind of student will the principal choose to be class president?

3. Who does the class president need to work with to do a good job?

4. Why can students choose a good class president?

5. Will students listen to a class president who they have not chosen?

Vocabulary Check

Complete each sentence with one of the words below.

obey	principal	select	staff	vote

1. Children should always _____ their parents' rules.

2. In South Korea, people _____ for a new president every five years.

3. The _____ at the computer store helped me solve a problem with my computer.

4. It is important to _____ a good name for your pet.

5. The leader of a school is called the _____.

Opinion Practice

Practice supporting and refuting the opinions below.

 Supporting Opinions

1. Principals will pick the students who will be the best class presidents…

2. Students will only vote for their friends…

3. Principals cannot pick the best class presidents…

4. It is important that students vote for their class president…

ⓐ because everybody can learn a lot about voting.

ⓑ because they do not know the students well.

ⓒ because they know which students can do the job well.

ⓓ because the friendships may end if they don't select them.

 Refuting Opinions

1. Students will pick the best class president.

2. It is a waste of time to have class elections. Students should be learning.

3. Principals may pick students who don't want to do the job.

4. The class teacher can tell the principal which student will be the best class president.

ⓐ This is unlikely. Principals have been teaching for many years. They know which students can be good class presidents.

ⓑ Not usually. Students usually pick the most popular student.

ⓒ I don't think so. The teacher will pick someone who he or she likes.

ⓓ That is incorrect. Students can learn many skills such as speech writing.

Opinion Examples

Read the opinions and answer the questions.

 Supporting Opinion

When it is time to choose a class president, the school principal should select the person. The first reason is that the principal will choose the student who can do the job the best. Principals and teachers have taught many children. As a result, they understand how students think and behave. The second reason is that everyone has a good chance of being the class leader. The principal will not choose the most popular student. He or she will select the student who can do the job well.

 Opposing Opinion

The class president should be chosen by the students. One reason is that principals will choose a person who they can control easily. Such class presidents cannot argue with the principal to make the school a better place. In addition, students can learn a lot during the process of voting for a class president. Students in the class can learn about writing speeches and public speaking. If the principal chooses the class leader, students will learn less.

1. Circle the main idea in each opinion.

2. Underline the supporting ideas in each opinion.

3. Can you think of some examples to support the ideas in each opinion?

Discussion Questions

Discuss these questions in groups.

1. Is it important to have a class president?

2. What type of student will be a good class president?

3. Do you think a principal will choose a student who he or she dislikes?

4. Do you think the class president, the principal, and the teacher should have a good relationship?

5. Do students learn many things from a class election? Or it is just a fun time when students don't have to study?

Let's Debate

Choose one of the statements below and then debate in groups.

1. The school principal should choose the class president.

2. The smartest student in class should be class president.

3. It is a waste of time to vote for a class president.

Unit 7
Are Fairy Tales Dangerous for Young Children?

People enjoyed fairy tales for hundreds of years. However, today's parents believe these stories are bad for their children. Are they correct?

Think of some fairy tales that you know about. Choose one that you like and one that you dislike. Explain your opinion about both stories.

A Fairy Tale That I Like...	
Title	
Reasons I Like It	

A Fairy Tale That I Dislike...	
Title	
Reasons I Dislike It	

Warm-Up Questions

1. Why do you think many children like fairy tales?

2. Do you think fairy tales are dangerous for young children?

3. Do you think children learn anything from fairy tales?

Are Fairy Tales Dangerous for Young Children?

As soon as children can understand simple stories, they read fairy tales. Most people believe that these stories are simple and fun. This idea may be wrong. Many parents now think that it is dangerous for children to read fairy tales.

Some people argue that children should not read fairy tales. One problem is that young children believe everything that they read. Many people and animals die in fairy tales. Young children will believe these things really happened. As a result, they will be upset. Another problem is that many fairy tales are scary. There are horrible characters that do bad things. This can frighten children and give them nightmares. Young children should not read about such scary events.

Other people argue that children should read fairy tales. The first benefit is that these stories help children to be creative. Many fairy tales take place in strange places. They also have strange characters in them. If children imagine the stories in their minds, they can become more creative. The second benefit is that fairy tales can teach children good lessons. When children read these stories, they can learn important life lessons.

Comprehension Check

Answer the questions using information from the reading passage.

1. What do most people think about fairy tales?

2. Why is it a problem that children believe what they read in fairy tales?

3. Why are young children scared when they read fairy tales?

4. Why can children be more creative if they read fairy tales?

5. How can learning about lessons in fairy tales benefit children?

Vocabulary Check

Complete each sentence with one of the words below.

creative	fairies	frighten	horrible	nightmare

1. It is easy to _____ my brother. I just need to tell him there is a spider on his clothes.

2. I am not a _____ person. I can never think of good ideas when I write a story.

3. It was really _____ when I saw a traffic accident.

4. My worst _____ is that I am falling down the stairs.

5. In stories, _____ have magic powers.

Opinion Practice

Practice supporting and refuting the opinions below.

 Supporting Opinions

1. Children who read fairy tales will improve their language skills...

2. It is dangerous for children to read fairy tales...

3. There may be some bad things in fairy tales, but young children don't notice them...

4. Fairy tales don't teach young children new ideas...

ⓐ because people wrote the stories many years ago.

ⓑ because they may do the bad things that they read about.

ⓒ because they will learn many new words.

ⓓ because they just understand the simple ideas of the stories.

 Refuting Opinions

1. Some fairy tales are too perfect. Everybody lives happily ever after.

2. Children will do the things that they read about in the fairy tales.

3. Young children will improve their language skills when they read fairy tales.

4. Young children will not understand any of the bad things in fairy tales.

ⓐ I don't think so. Parents will not allow their children to do bad things.

ⓑ I disagree. They can understand a lot of things. For example, they understand that people die.

ⓒ This is not a problem. Young children should read stories with happy endings.

ⓓ I don't think so. Most fairy tales contain words that people do not use anymore. Such words will not improve language skills.

Opinion Examples

Read the opinions and answer the questions.

 Supporting Opinion

 20 / Unit 7

It is a very bad idea for children to read fairy tales. One danger is that children will not learn new ideas. In these stories, women do the housework and men are heroes. These are not new ideas. Another danger is that these stories always have a happy ending. It is a problem because young children will think that everything in life will always be perfect. This is not true. In fact, life is difficult and many things go wrong.

 Opposing Opinion

 21 / Unit 7

Young children should read fairy tales. One reason is that fairy tales are a great way for young children to improve their language skills. Often, children do not like to read, but they enjoy fairy tales. As a result, they can improve their vocabulary and grammar skills. Another reason is that young children don't understand everything that they read. They just try to understand the main ideas. As a result, children will not learn about any of the bad things that are contained in fairy tales.

1. Circle the main idea in each opinion.

2. Underline the supporting ideas in each opinion.

3. Can you think of some examples to support the ideas in each opinion?

Discussion Questions

Discuss these questions in groups.

1. Do you think children learn any bad things when they read fairy tales?

2. Are fairy tales better than other stories? Why?

3. Do you think children will do the things that they read in fairy tales?

4. Is it a problem if all fairy tales have a happy ending?

5. Are fairy tales a good way for children to learn life lessons?

Let's Debate

Choose one of the statements below and then debate in groups.

1. It is dangerous for young children to read fairy tales.

2. Fairy tales are not useful because they are too old.

3. New stories are much better than fairy tales.

Unit 8
Banning Bottled Water

Some schools in the United States have banned the sale of bottled water. Many parents and teachers have welcomed this decision. Will it be a good idea if Korean schools stop selling bottled water?

 **Look at the list of drinks below. Decide which are the best drinks and which are the healthiest. Write your answers in the two columns below. Discuss your answers with other students.**

| Coke | Orange Juice | Coffee | Water | Milk |

Best Drink	Healthiest Drink

Warm-Up Questions

1. Why do you think people buy bottled water?

2. Where can students get bottled water if they cannot buy it in school?

3. Do you drink bottled water or other soft drinks? Why?

DC3-08
MP3

Banning Bottled Water

In 1989, some companies put water into plastic bottles for the first time. Many people liked these products, and bottled water became popular. These days, millions of people all over the world enjoy bottled water. However, some schools have stopped selling it. Is this a good thing?

Some people argue that it is a great idea to ban the sale of bottled water. One reason is that bottled water is bad for our environment. We use so much plastic for the bottles, and then we just throw them away. We also need to use a lot of water to clean the plastic bottles. Another problem is that bottled water is very expensive. It is such a waste of money when we can get water from the faucet for a very low price.

Other people argue that bottled water has many benefits. First, bottled water is healthy. It is much better for students to buy water than to buy sodas and fruit juices. These drinks contain lots of sugar and other additives, such as unnatural flavors and colors. Second, when we buy bottled water, we know that it will be clean and of good

quality. When we drink from a water fountain, we don't know if it has been purified. In other words, we don't know if they have removed dirty substances from the water.

Comprehension Check

Answer the questions using information from the reading passage.

1. Why did bottled water become popular in 1989?

2. Why is bottled water bad for the environment?

3. Why is it a waste of money to buy bottled water?

4. Why is it much better for students to buy bottled water instead of sodas or fruit juices?

5. What is the reason that people don't drink water from a water fountain?

Vocabulary Check

Complete each sentence with one of the words below.

additives	banned	faucet	purified	remove

1. The cleaner can _____ any kinds of stains.

2. My kitchen became full of water when I broke the _____.

3. We shouldn't drink water from a lake because it has not been _____.

4. Food companies use a lot of _____ to make their snacks taste great.

5. The government _____ the sale of tiger skin to protect tigers.

Opinion Practice

Practice supporting and refuting the opinions below.

Supporting Opinions

1. Bottled water is very bad for the environment…

2. Schools don't need to sell bottled water…

3. Many students don't want to use water fountains…

4. Students should be allowed to buy bottled water…

ⓐ because they need to carry it around with them.

ⓑ because a lot of fuel is used to transport the water all over the world.

ⓒ because there are many water fountains that students can use.

ⓓ because they think that they are dirty and unhealthy.

Refuting Opinions

1. Students need to buy bottled water because they don't have time to line up at the water fountain.

2. Bottled water is of higher quality.

3. Bottled water causes too much pollution.

4. Bottled water is too expensive.

ⓐ I disagree. There are many ways to recycle plastic bottles.

ⓑ That is not true. Students don't have to line up and wait because schools have many water fountains.

ⓒ I disagree. Bottled water is usually much cheaper than other soft drinks.

ⓓ That is not true. Water from the faucet is of higher quality than bottled water because the government spends a lot of money cleaning the water.

Opinion Examples

Read the opinions and answer the questions.

 Supporting Opinion

Schools should ban the sale of bottled water. The first reason is that water from the faucet is very clean. It is much cleaner than bottled water. This is because the government spends a lot of money purifying the water. As a result, people cannot tell the difference between tap water and bottled water. Another reason is that bottled water is bad for the environment. Large trucks and airplanes transport bottled water. They use a lot of fuel and cause pollution. It does not make sense to transport bottled water to different countries.

 Opposing Opinion

Schools should continue to sell bottled water. First, bottled water is not that expensive. It is usually much cheaper than other soft drinks. Also, we can reuse the plastic bottles many times. That will help to save money. Second, it is not a good idea to ban only bottled water. All soft drinks cause a lot of pollution because they also use plastic, metal, and glass. These drinks cause much more pollution than bottled water. They are also unhealthy. Schools should ban soft drinks and keep selling bottled water.

1. Circle the main idea in each opinion.

2. Underline the supporting ideas in each opinion.

3. Can you think of some examples to support the ideas in each opinion?

Discussion Questions

Discuss these questions in groups.

1. Do you think bottled water will be popular if all the bottles are made from glass?

2. Should we buy bottled water that comes from a different country?

3. Do you think that bottled water is too expensive?

4. How do you feel about using water fountains at school?

5. Do you think bottled water tastes better than tap water?

Let's Debate

Choose one of the statements below and then debate in groups.

1. Schools should ban the sale of bottled water.

2. All students should bring their own reusable bottles of water to school.

3. The government should ban bottled water from a different country.

Unit 9
Is Hacking a Problem?

These days, we use the Internet to do many things. We visit many different websites to buy products and join organizations. This means that we have a lot of information online. Is it a problem if people hack those websites?

Look at the different types of information below. Then, order the information according to its importance (1 is the most important, 4 is the least important). Explain why you have chosen this order.

Your Name and Date of Birth	Your Bank Account Details
Your Address	Your Online Game Details

	Type of Information	Reasons
1.		
2.		
3.		
4.		

Warm-Up Questions

1. What do you think hacking is?

2. Why do people hack websites?

3. Is hacking easy to do?

Is Hacking a Problem?

These days, there always seems to be a story about hacking in the news. Many people say that hackers are bad because they steal information from individuals and companies. Is hacking really a problem, though?

Some people argue that hacking is a problem. One reason why hacking is bad is that it is illegal. We are not allowed to steal people's information from computers or online accounts. Another problem with hacking is that people don't trust the Internet. They worry that hackers will steal all their money. They don't want to buy products online. If these things continue to happen, we won't be able to use the Internet anymore.

Other people argue that hacking is helpful. Hackers find security problems that companies have. They tell the companies about such problems. As a result, these businesses can improve their Internet security. This helps to keep customers' information much safer. In addition, many hackers are very smart. They like to improve computer games or other products. This can benefit companies because they have better products to sell.

Comprehension Check

Answer the questions using information from the reading passage.

1. Why do many people say that hackers are bad?

2. Where can hackers steal people's information from?

3. Why is it a problem that people don't trust the Internet?

4. It is helpful for hackers to find problems with a company' Internet security. Why?

5. Why may companies like people hacking their games and products?

Vocabulary Check

Complete each sentence with one of the words below.

illegal	improve	security	smart	steal

1. My friends think I am _____ because I got the highest test score.

2. The best way to _____ your English is to practice a lot.

3. It is wrong to _____ other people's things.

4. The website _____ system was so bad that it got hacked.

5. If something is _____, we are not allowed to do it.

Opinion Practice

Practice supporting and refuting the opinions below.

Supporting Opinions

1. Hacking stops people from trusting the Internet…

2. People should not hack websites…

3. Hackers can help make the world better…

4. We need to have hackers…

ⓐ because they give us information about bad people.

ⓑ because they worry that hackers will steal their information.

ⓒ because it is illegal.

ⓓ because they know how to create strong security systems.

Refuting Opinions

1. All hackers are bad people.

2. Companies dislike hackers.

3. Hackers find a lot of information about bad people and bad companies.

4. Hacking is a great skill.

ⓐ I disagree. Many companies like hackers because they tell the companies about problems with their products.

ⓑ I disagree. Hacking is dangerous because it can be used to cause many problems.

ⓒ That is not true. Hackers just try to make a lot of money by hacking websites. They are not interested in finding information about bad people.

ⓓ That is not true. Many people who hack do it because they want to make the Internet safer.

Opinion Examples

Read the opinions and answer the questions.

 Supporting Opinion

 **26** / Unit 9

Hacking is a serious problem. One reason is that people don't want to use the Internet. They are worried that hackers will steal their information. This is a big problem. The Internet is so helpful, but people who are scared to use it will not experience it. Another reason is that hacking is illegal. Hacking means breaking into someone's computer system and stealing information. This is a crime and we should stop it.

 Opposing Opinion

 **27** / Unit 9

Hacking is not a problem. It can really help everyone. First, most people hack websites to test how good their security systems are. If they find problems, they tell the companies. Then the companies can fix the problems. As a result, the Internet and computers will be much safer. Another benefit is that hackers can find information about bad people or companies. They tell the police about those criminals or companies. As a result, hackers can stop criminals from doing bad things.

1. Circle the main idea in each opinion.

2. Underline the supporting ideas in each opinion.

3. Can you think of some examples to support the ideas in each opinion?

Discussion Questions

Discuss these questions in groups.

1. Is hacking a good thing if you don't steal any information?

2. Do you feel scared to use the Internet because of hackers?

3. Do you want to learn how to hack websites?

4. Do you think hackers should go to jail?

5. How will you feel if someone hacks your computer?

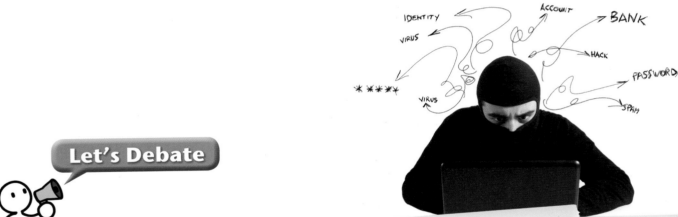

Let's Debate

Choose one of the statements below and then debate in groups.

1. Hacking is very bad for our world.

2. Schools should teach students how to hack websites.

3. Hacking is okay if the government allows it.

Unit 10
We Should Ban Private Education

Many students in South Korea go to private academies after school. Will this help the students? Or does it cause too many problems for the students and their parents?

Imagine that you are going to open a private academy. You want to teach students something that they will like. And you want them to enjoy coming to your academy. How will you achieve this? Complete the table below and discuss your answers with other students.

Name of Your Academy:

	Answer	Why Students Will Like It
What will you teach?		
What homework will you give?		
What will you give students so that they like your academy?		

Warm-Up Questions

1. Why should we educate children?

2. What do you think about private education?

3. Why do you think so many Koreans attend private academies?

We Should Ban Private Education

Imagine learning more challenging subjects after studying hard at school all day. For many students in South Korea, this happens every day. But do we really need private education?

Some people argue that we should ban private education because it is unnecessary. One reason is that children will be too fatigued. In other words, they will be very tired. Students go to school for many hours each day. When they go to private academies, they are too tired to study well. Many students usually fall asleep or feel stressed. Another reason is that many successful countries don't have private academies. For example, students in Finland do not have private education, but they are some of the smartest students in the world.

Other people argue that private education has many benefits. Students who attend private academies improve much faster. They know much more than other students. These students get to study more subjects and learn them in more detail. Another benefit of private education is that students

can have more time with the teacher. The class sizes of private academies are much smaller than those of regular schools. As a result, students can get help when they are stuck.

Comprehension Check

Answer the questions using information from the reading passage.

1. Why are students who go to private academies too tired?

2. What usually happens when students attend private academies?

3. Do all successful countries have private education?

4. Why do students who attend private academies improve faster and know more?

5. Why can students at private academies get more help?

Vocabulary Check

Complete each sentence with one of the words below.

challenging	detail	fatigued	regular	stuck

1. Climbing Mount Everest is very _____.

2. The smart student wants to learn the topic in more _____.

3. Melissa was really _____ after studying for eight hours.

4. Compared with private academies, _____ schools do not have many teachers.

5. The math question was very difficult. I was _____ for a long time before I got the right answer.

Opinion Practice

Practice supporting and refuting the opinions below.

 Supporting Opinions

1. It is not fair to have private education…

2. Students who attend private academies can learn more…

3. Private academies stop children from being active…

4. Parents want private education for their children…

ⓐ because they are too busy to do any exercise.

ⓑ because some students cannot afford to attend private academies.

ⓒ because many of the teachers are experts in their subjects.

ⓓ because they think regular schools are not good enough.

 Refuting Opinions

1. Private academies have much better classrooms.

2. Korean students will be too tired to study at private academies.

3. The class sizes of private academies are much smaller than those of regular schools.

4. Students don't enjoy studying in private academies.

ⓐ I don't think so. Many private academies have hundreds of students in one class.

ⓑ I don't think so. Many schools have modern classrooms and computers. These classrooms are better than those of private academies.

ⓒ This is not true. Students can be more creative in private academies. As a result, they enjoy studying there.

ⓓ This is not true. Korean students don't become tired at school because they do not study at all.

Opinion Examples

Read the opinions and answer the questions.

 Supporting Opinion

 **29** / Unit 10

We should ban private education. The first reason is that it is not fair. Parents need to pay for their children to go to private academies. Some parents cannot afford the fees. As a result, children who cannot attend private classes will learn less and get lower test scores. This can stop them from being successful. Another reason that we should not allow private education is that many regular schools have very good classrooms. Students can learn in a great environment at school, and they won't be fatigued.

 Opposing Opinion

 **30** / Unit 10

We should allow private education. Many parents don't think that their children's education at regular schools is good. Therefore, they want their children to have private education so that they can learn as much as possible. In fact, private education is the reason why South Korean students have become so smart. Another great thing about private academies is that students can do more creative and interesting activities. Students enjoy learning when they can do experiments or use their imagination.

1. Circle the main idea in each opinion.

2. Underline the supporting ideas in each opinion.

3. Can you think of some examples to support the ideas in each opinion?

Discussion Questions

Discuss these questions in groups.

1. Do you think it is a problem if some students cannot afford private education?

2. Do you think students who go to private academies learn more?

3. What do your parents think about regular schools? Do they think that you learn enough?

4. Is it better to learn in a classroom in a regular school or in a classroom at a private academy?

5. Do you like to be in a class with a few students? Or do you prefer a class with many students?

Let's Debate

Choose one of the statements below and then debate in groups.

1. We should ban private education.

2. Students should not have private education in vacations.

3. It is better to learn in a class with fewer students.

Unit 11
Being a Vegetarian

Everybody needs to eat. We hear that we should eat lots of vegetables and fruits to stay healthy. However, should we eat meat? Will it be better if we become vegetarians?

Imagine that you are going to eat only vegetarian foods for one month. What do you think are the advantages and disadvantages of this? List your ideas below.

Advantages of a Vegetarian Diet	Disadvantages of a Vegetarian Diet

Warm-Up Questions

1. Do you like to eat meat? Why? Why not?

2. Will you stop eating meat if it is bad for you?

3. Will you eat meat if you have to kill the animal yourself?

Being a Vegetarian

Steak, chicken, bulgogi, and samgyeopsal are just some of the meat that we can eat if we want to. Eating meat is very popular all around the world. But will it be much better for us and the planet if we stop consuming animals?

Some people argue that if we no longer eat meat, there will be many benefits. The first benefit is that humans will be healthier. Vegetarians are less obese. As a result, they are less likely to suffer from diseases. Just by not eating meat, we will be less likely to get sick. Another benefit is that we will stop killing millions of animals each year. It is horrible to kill animals because they have feelings. Animals such as pigs and ducks can feel happiness, sadness, and pain.

Other people argue that there are many great things about eating meat. People who eat meat can benefit from the nutrients and vitamins. Meat helps us to be stronger and fitter. Many vegetarians are skinny and weak. This is because it is difficult to get enough nutrients from their meatless diets. Another great thing about meat is that it tastes great. We need to eat, so we should consume foods that are delicious. A vegetarian diet is very bland. In other words, it does not taste good. We will get bored with this diet.

Comprehension Check

Answer the questions using information from the reading passage.

1. What are some of the meat that we can eat?

2. Why are vegetarians healthier?

3. Why is it horrible to kill animals?

4. What health benefits do meat eaters have?

5. Why is it not fun to eat a vegetarian diet?

Vocabulary Check

Complete each sentence with one of the words below.

bland	consume	nutrients	planet	vegetarian

1. The _____ we live on is called Earth.

2. A _____ diet does not include meat or fish.

3. People in rich countries _____ too much food.

4. Protein and vitamins are examples of _____ .

5. A _____ diet does not contain much spice.

Opinion Practice

Practice supporting and refuting the opinions below.

Supporting Opinions

1. It is much safer to eat a vegetarian diet…

2. People with active jobs need to eat meat…

3. Our bodies need meat…

4. It is better for the world if people become vegetarians…

ⓐ because we have been eating meat for thousands of years.

ⓑ because there is less chance of getting food poisoning.

ⓒ because they need a lot of energy to do their work well.

ⓓ because growing plants is much better for the environment.

Refuting Opinions

1. Our environment will be cleaner if we are all vegetarians.

2. Meat is good for our health.

3. Vegetarians will not get enough protein and other nutrients.

4. It is horrible to kill animals for meat.

ⓐ I disagree. The animals don't know what is happening, and they don't feel any pain.

ⓑ This is incorrect. They can get lots of protein and other nutrients from milk, cheese, and eggs.

ⓒ I disagree. Meat contains unhealthy fats, and they are bad for our health.

ⓓ This is incorrect. If we are all vegetarians, animals will make our environment dirty.

Opinion Examples

Read the opinions and answer the questions.

 Supporting Opinion

People should stop eating meat and become vegetarians. One reason is that a vegetarian diet is much safer. Meat eaters are more likely to get food poisoning because the meat is not fresh or not cooked correctly. Vegetarians don't have this problem because they can clean fruits and vegetables very easily. Another reason is that vegetarians can still get all the nutrients that their bodies need. As a result, these people are much healthier than meat eaters. They will have a better lifestyle.

 Opposing Opinion

People should continue to eat meat. To begin with, people are very busy these days. So, they need to eat foods that give them energy. Rice and vegetables are great foods, but we need to eat them with meat. If we don't eat meat, we will be hungry very quickly and have no energy. In addition, people understand that animals have feelings. Therefore, there are laws to make sure that animals have a happy life before we eat them. In fact, many animals live very happy and natural lives before they die.

1. Circle the main idea in each opinion.

2. Underline the supporting ideas in each opinion.

3. Can you think of some examples to support the ideas in each opinion?

Discussion Questions

Discuss these questions in groups.

1. Do you enjoy eating meat?

2. Is it important that farm animals have a happy life?

3. Do you want to be a vegetarian?

4. Do you think it is easy to be a vegetarian in Korea? Why?

5. Do you think vegetarians are healthier than meat eaters?

Choose one of the statements below and then debate in groups.

1. All of us should become vegetarians.

2. People should have at least one meat-free day a week.

3. We should continue to consume animal products.

Unit 12
Leaving School at a Younger Age

All children in Korea need to go to school. Most students study until they finish high school. Will it be better if more students leave school when they are younger and get a job?

Think about the benefits of staying in school and the benefits of getting a job. List your ideas in the table below.

Benefits of Being in School	Benefits of Having a Job

Warm-Up Questions

1. What is the best age for a person to start working full-time? Why?

2. Do you think many fifteen-year-olds want to finish school and start working?

3. Will your parents be happy if you leave school at fifteen?

DC3-12
MP3

Leaving School at a Younger Age

South Korean students are required to attend school until they are fifteen. But most students continue studying for much longer. Many students don't benefit from going to high school and university. Leaving school and learning a trade may be much better.

Some people argue that it will be helpful for students to finish school at fifteen. One reason is that many students find it difficult to study. Or they just dislike studying. It is very stressful for them to go to school. These children will be much happier if they are trained to do a job. Another reason is that classes will be better. Teenagers who don't like school usually misbehave or cause problems. When they leave school, the remaining students will behave sensibly.

Other people argue that students should not leave school at fifteen. First, the students are too young to go to a company to work. They are just children. Learning to do a real job will be too tough, so the teenagers will probably quit. Second, students need to learn many skills so that they can be successful when they are older. The best way to learn new skills is to study at school. Students who leave at fifteen will not know much.

Comprehension Check

Answer the questions using information from the reading passage.

1. At what age can students leave school if they want to?

2. How will students who don't like studying feel if they have to go to school?

3. Why will classes be better when the students who don't like them leave?

4. What will happen if teenagers start training to do a real job?

5. What is the best way to learn new skills?

Vocabulary Check

Complete each sentence with one of the words below.

misbehaved	required	tough	trade	trained

1. It is very _____ to run a marathon.

2. In the past, most people learned a _____ such as hairdressing.

3. His father didn't allow him to play outside because he _____ at school.

4. Police officers are _____ to catch criminals.

5. If you want to drive a car, you are _____ to get a driver's license.

Opinion Practice

Practice supporting and refuting the opinions below.

Supporting Opinions

1. It is a bad idea for teenagers to choose a job when they are fifteen…

2. Teenagers who learn a trade can earn a lot of money when they are older…

3. Students need to learn many different subjects…

4. Some students need to leave school at fifteen…

(a) because they will have a lot of experience and be good at their jobs.

(b) because they may want to have a different job a few years later.

(c) because they need to earn money for their families.

(d) because they can do many different jobs when they are older.

Refuting Opinions

1. Students shouldn't leave school when they are fifteen. This is because they don't know what they want to do when they are older.

2. If more teenagers learn a trade, everybody will have a job.

3. Teenagers are too young to start working for a company.

4. Many students find it difficult to study. Learning a trade will be much better.

(a) I disagree. Everybody will have a job if they continue to study and learn.

(b) I don't think so. Most students find it easy to study school subjects.

(c) I disagree. Many teenagers already know what they want to do in life.

(d) I don't think so. Teenagers can do many different jobs in a company. They will also learn new skills very quickly.

Opinion Examples

Read the opinions and answer the questions.

 Supporting Opinion

 35 / Unit 12

It will be a great idea for many students who hate school to leave at fifteen. One reason is that the teenagers can get a job and a lot of training from a company. These young workers will learn good skills and will have a great job. Another reason is that teenagers will become adults much faster. Adults are responsible for their behavior. Teenagers working for a company will learn to behave responsibly. Students at school cannot learn to be responsible for their behavior.

 Opposing Opinion

 36 / Unit 12

It is a bad idea for any student to leave school at fifteen. To begin with, these children are too young to know what job they want to do when they are older. Most students change their minds many times before they decide on a job. Students who choose a job at fifteen will soon be very unhappy. Another problem is that some students need more time to develop learning skills. If the teenagers continue studying at school, they will find learning much easier.

1. Circle the main idea in each opinion.

2. Underline the supporting ideas in each opinion.

3. Can you think of some examples to support the ideas in each opinion?

Discussion Questions

Discuss these questions in groups.

1. Can teenagers choose a good job when they are fifteen?

2. Do you think that we can become better at learning when we are older?

3. Do students need to stay in school and learn many different subjects? Why?

4. Can fifteen-year-olds work in a company with adults?

5. Will teenagers learn more skills at school or at work?

Let's Debate

Choose one of the statements below and then debate in groups.

1. It is better for many students to finish school at fifteen and get a job.

2. Every student should study until they finish university.

3. Becoming an expert at one subject is better than studying many different subjects.

Unit 13
Banning Child Beauty Contests

A beauty contest is an event where judges decide which person is the most beautiful. The winner usually gets a great prize. There are now many beauty contests for children. Is this a good idea?

Some people like beauty contests, while others dislike them. Think about some good and bad things about beauty contests. Write them in the table below. Discuss your answers with your classmates.

Good Things About Beauty Contests	Bad Things About Beauty Contests

Warm-Up Questions

1. Do you want to go to a beauty contest? Why?

2. Do you think beauty contests are important?

3. What makes somebody beautiful?

Banning Child Beauty Contests

Children wear make-up, show their talents, and give speeches in child beauty contests. These days, some governments want to ban these contests for children under sixteen. What do you think?

Some people argue that the government should ban child beauty contests. These contests teach children that their appearance is the most important thing. They will worry too much about how they look. However, a child's personality is much more important. In addition, children who take part in beauty contests don't have a happy childhood. They are too busy thinking about how they look and memorizing the things they will say to the audience. But children should only think about studying and playing.

Other people argue that the government should not ban child beauty contests. Children can learn many important talents. They can learn how to speak to many people and how to dance. These are skills that can help the children become successful. In addition, children can have a lot of fun. It is great to wear nice clothes and to sing songs to an audience. Other children who do not take part in beauty contests will just sit at home and play computer games.

Comprehension Check

Answer the questions using information from the reading passage.

1. What kinds of things do children do in beauty contests?

2. Why will children who take part in beauty contests worry about how they look?

3. Why won't children who enter beauty contests have a happy childhood?

4. Why is it good for children to learn many different talents?

5. Children will have a lot of fun when they take part in beauty contests. Why?

Vocabulary Check

Complete each sentence with one of the words below.

audience	personality	childhood	appearance	memorize

1. My grandmother's _____ was very short. She started work when she was twelve.

2. I have to _____ 20 words each day for my vocabulary test at school.

3. The musician was angry with the _____ because they were talking on their cellphones.

4. It is important to think about our _____. If we don't look good, it can be hard to get a good job.

5. My _____ is very different from that of my brother. I am quiet, but he is loud.

Opinion Practice

Practice supporting and refuting the opinions below.

Supporting Opinions

1. Taking part in beauty contests is a great way to meet new friends…

2. Many parents want their children to enter beauty contests…

3. Beauty contests are too expensive…

4. It is a good experience for children to enter beauty contests…

   ⓐ because parents need to pay for dresses, haircuts, and lessons for their children.

   ⓑ because the children will like similar things.

   ⓒ because they believe that such contests will help their children to succeed.

   ⓓ because they will learn that they need to organize their time and work hard.

Refuting Opinions

1. Beauty contests are not bad. They are just like sports because there will always be losers.

2. It is too stressful for children to perform in front of a big audience.

3. Children who enter beauty contests can become good friends.

4. Children who take part in beauty contests will not enjoy their childhood.

   ⓐ I disagree. It is difficult to be friends with people who we are trying to beat. Children in beauty contests will feel lonely.

   ⓑ I disagree. Children can become better at sports, but they cannot become prettier.

   ⓒ I don't think so. Many children will really enjoy learning how to sing, model, and dance. They will have a great childhood.

   ⓓ I don't think so. After performing a few times, children will not feel stressed. In fact, many really enjoy being on stage.

Opinion Examples

Read the opinions and answer the questions.

 Supporting Opinion

The government should ban child beauty contests immediately. The first reason is that parents force their children to take part in those contests. Many parents think that their daughters will be successful in the future if they win many contests. However, the children usually feel very sad and stressed. The second reason is that these contests are too expensive. Families need to pay for the entrance fees, clothes, lessons, and beauty treatments. Some families spend so much money on these contests that they don't save any cash for the future.

 Opposing Opinion

Beauty contests are not dangerous. In fact, they are enjoyable. One reason is that children can have a great time learning how to sing, dance, and model. Also, they get the chance to wear many beautiful clothes. These are the things that many young girls really like to do. Another reason is that entering a beauty contest is a great experience. It is fun to learn how to speak and perform in front of many people. In fact, these are skills that can help children to get good jobs when they are older.

1. Circle the main idea in each opinion.

2. Underline the supporting ideas in each opinion.

3. Can you think of some examples to support the ideas in each opinion?

Discussion Questions

Discuss these questions in groups.

1. Which should be more important in a beauty contest: appearance or talent?

2. Do you think children who enter beauty contests can be friends with each other?

3. Do you think that children who enter beauty contests learn useful skills?

4. Is it okay for parents to spend a lot of money so that their children can enter beauty contests?

5. Can children who spend a lot of time practicing for beauty contests do well in school?

Let's Debate

Choose one of the statements below and then debate in groups.

1. The government should ban child beauty contests right away.

2. There is no difference between child beauty contests and competitive sports.

3. Parents should never force their children to enter beauty contests.

Unit 14
Living in a Rural or Urban Area

In the past, most people in Korea lived in the countryside. These days, however, most Koreans live in cities. Are urban areas better places? Where do you want to live?

Think about the similarities and differences between living in a rural area and living in an urban area. Write your ideas in the Venn diagram below. Talk about your answers with your partner.

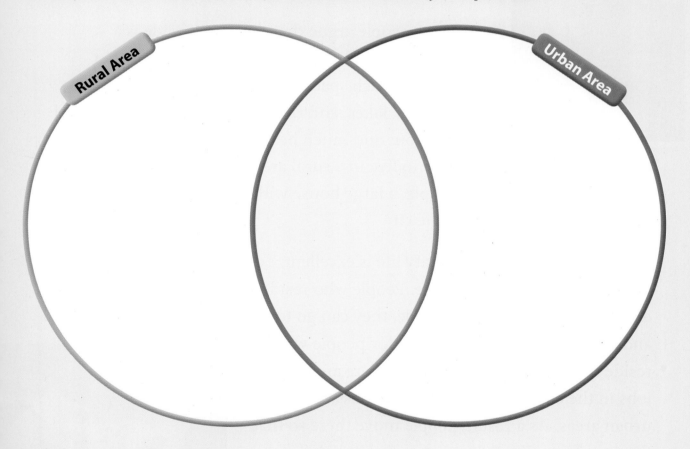

Rural Area

Urban Area

Warm-Up Questions

1. Why do you think so many people want to live in the city?

2. Do you think it is good to live in the city?

3. What fun things can you do in the countryside?

Living in a Rural or Urban Area

The number of people living in cities is growing all the time. Over 80% of South Koreans live in urban areas. However, some people are moving back to the countryside. Is it better to live in a rural or urban area?

Some people argue that the countryside is a wonderful place to reside. The first reason is that there is so much space. Rural areas have many fields, mountains, lakes, and rivers. People who live here feel less anxious and much healthier. The second reason is that it is much less expensive to live in a rural area. Accommodations and foods are cheaper. For example, a large house with a garden is often cheaper than a small apartment in the city.

Other people argue that city life is excellent. To begin with, urban areas are very exciting places to live. People who reside in cities can do something different every day. For instance, they can go to museums, movie theaters, and concerts. This is impossible for people who reside in rural areas. In addition, there are many jobs in the city. In fact, all the best jobs are in urban areas. As a result, people move there so that they can be successful.

Comprehension Check

Answer the questions using information from the reading passage.

1. What percent of South Koreans live in urban areas?

2. Why is there a lot of space in rural areas?

3. What things are cheaper in rural areas?

4. Why are urban areas exciting places to live?

5. Why do people move to urban areas?

Vocabulary Check

Complete each sentence with one of the words below.

accommodations	anxious	impossible	reside	urban

1. When I'm older, I will _____ by the ocean.

2. I feel very _____ when there are too many people in the room.

3. _____ problems affect cities and the people living in them.

4. In many cities, it is very difficult to find _____ .

5. It is _____ for humans to visit the sun.

Opinion Practice

Practice supporting and refuting the opinions below.

 Supporting Opinions

1. Traveling in the city is very easy…

2. People who live in the city can have more privacy…

3. The countryside is much cleaner…

4. It is much easier to sleep in rural areas…

ⓐ because there are fewer factories, cars, and people.

ⓑ because there is so much public transportation.

ⓒ because it is really dark and nobody makes noise.

ⓓ because nobody knows who they are.

Refuting Opinions

1. It is less stressful to live in the countryside.

2. The countryside is a great place for families to live.

3. Cities are better places to live because there are so many things to do.

4. There are so many kinds of foods to choose from in the city.

ⓐ I disagree. People living in cities usually do only a few things, and there are not many exciting activities.

ⓑ I disagree. There are fewer jobs and services in the countryside. That is stressful.

ⓒ I don't think so. Children will get very bored in the countryside. They will be unhappy, and their families will also feel unhappy.

ⓓ I don't think so. Not many restaurants in the city give us many kinds of foods.

Opinion Examples

Read the opinions and answer the questions.

 Supporting Opinion

 **41** / Unit 14

It is much better to live in an urban area. The first reason is that it is so easy to travel. Residents can use buses, trains, subways, or taxis. Public transportation in cities is cheap and can be used day and night. However, the countryside has very bad public transportation, and everyone needs to use their cars to travel. The second reason is that people who live in cities can have more privacy. It is much better when people don't know everything about us. In rural areas, there are not many people and everyone knows everything about each other.

 Opposing Opinion

 **42** / Unit 14

It is much better to live in a rural area. The main reason is that the countryside is much cleaner than the city. There are fewer factories, cars, and people. As a result, there is very little pollution. This is much healthier than living in dirty cities. Another reason is that the countryside is more relaxing. It is much quieter and much darker at nighttime. People who live in the countryside can sleep really well and have much more energy. People who get enough rest are less likely to get sick, too. It is much healthier for people to live in the countryside.

1. Circle the main idea in each opinion.

2. Underline the supporting ideas in each opinion.

3. Can you think of some examples to support the ideas in each opinion?

Discussion Questions

Discuss these questions in groups.

1. Do you like taking the bus in the city? Or do you prefer using your car in the countryside?

2. Which is more important: having a good job or living in a clean environment?

3. Do you want to live in a larger house in the countryside? Or do you prefer living in a modern apartment in the city?

4. Do you think it is easier for people to rest in the countryside? Why?

5. People who live in the city don't know many people, but people who live in the countryside know many people. Which is better?

Let's Debate

Choose one of the statements below and then debate in groups.

1. It is much better to live in a rural area.

2. It is better for families with young children to live in the city.

3. In the future, more people will live in the countryside.

Unit 15
Korean Celebrities and Military Service

All healthy Korean men must do military service before they are 35 years old. But some people say that celebrities do not have to do military service. What do you think?

Think about what you have heard and seen about soldiers. Imagine what a typical day may be like for people doing military service.

Activity	Time of Day	Details
Waking Up		
Morning Activities		
Lunch		
Afternoon Activities		
Dinner		
Evening Activities		
Bedtime		

Warm-Up Questions

1. Why do you think South Korea has military service?

2. Do you want to do military service?

3. What do you think is the hardest thing about doing military service?

DC3-15
MP3

Korean Celebrities and Military Service

South Korea has become one of the most developed countries in the world. However, because of North Korea, South Korea needs all young men to complete military service. Should Korean celebrities also be required to do so?

Some people argue that celebrities should do military training because every Korean has a duty to help the country. In fact, there are people who are more important than celebrities, such as scientists and doctors. These people have to complete military service. In addition, famous people who become real soldiers or sailors will be very popular. Therefore, they can have very successful careers after they have finished their military service.

Other people argue that Korean stars don't have to do military service. One reason is that celebrities' careers are very short. After spending two years doing military service, they may not be popular or get a bad injury. Another reason is that celebrities and sports stars give a lot of happiness to the Korean people. The celebrities should continue to entertain the country instead of doing military jobs that anybody can do.

Comprehension Check

Answer the questions using information from the reading passage.

1. Why does South Korea need all young men to do military service?

2. Which jobs are more important than being a celebrity?

3. Why may celebrities benefit if they complete their military service?

4. Why is it a problem that celebrities' careers are very short?

5. How do Korean celebrities benefit the country's citizens?

Vocabulary Check

Complete each sentence with one of the words below.

celebrities	completed	developed	duty	entertain

1. Canada is one of the most _____ countries in the world.

2. _____ often appear on television, so everybody knows many things about them.

3. Parents have a _____ to look after their children.

4. Some good ways to _____ young children is by playing games or watching movies.

5. We have _____ the task within seven days.

Opinion Practice

Practice supporting and refuting the opinions below.

Supporting Opinions

1. Every Korean male celebrity should do military service…

2. Celebrities cannot do military training well…

3. It is better for South Korea if celebrities don't become soldiers…

4. Korean stars will become more popular if they do military service…

   ⓐ because their jobs create a lot of money for the country.

   ⓑ because more people will respect them.

   ⓒ because other ordinary people will always bother them for autographs.

   ⓓ because it is the duty of Korean citizens.

Refuting Opinions

1. Korean stars may get hurt during military service.

2. Celebrities will still be popular after they finish their military training.

3. Famous people usually have short careers. They shouldn't do military service.

4. Celebrities are not special. They are just famous for doing something well.

   ⓐ I don't think so. Many celebrities have long careers. Also, people who have short careers should do military service.

   ⓑ I don't think so. The military try to keep everybody safe.

   ⓒ I disagree. Celebrities are special because they can do many great things. Ordinary people cannot do those things.

   ⓓ I disagree. After two years, people will have forgotten about the celebrities.

Opinion Examples

Read the opinions and answer the questions.

 Supporting Opinion

 **.MP3** 44 / Unit 15

Korean celebrities should do military service. The first reason is that celebrities are not more special than ordinary people. Every healthy man needs to complete military service, so famous people need to do their duty as Koreans, too. The second reason is that Korean celebrities who complete real military training become more popular. This is because their fans and other citizens will respect them. As a result, these celebrities can be even more successful.

 Opposing Opinion

 **.MP3** 45 / Unit 15

Famous Koreans don't have to do military service. To begin with, these celebrities can benefit Korea more when they do their usual jobs. Famous Korean singers, actors, and sports players can help foreigners learn more about Korea. Fans from different countries may even visit Korea and spend money. In addition, celebrities' careers are usually very short. After they finish their military service, they may not be popular anymore and lose their jobs.

1. Circle the main idea in each opinion.

2. Underline the supporting ideas in each opinion.

3. Can you think of some examples to support the ideas in each opinion?

Discussion Questions

Discuss these questions in groups.

1. What do you think about Korean celebrities who don't do military service?

2. Should Korean stars do the same training as other Korean people?

3. Does it bother you when you cannot see your favorite Korean celebrity because he is doing military service?

4. Korean sports stars who win important sports competitions don't have to do military service. Do you agree with this?

5. Should Korean celebrities do military service if it means that Korea will be less rich?

Let's Debate

Choose one of the statements below and then debate in groups.

1. Korean celebrities should complete military service.

2. No Korean men have to complete military service.

3. Korean women have to do military service.

Unit 16
Renewable Energy

Most of our energy comes from fossil fuels such as oil and gas. However, they cause many problems. Is it time for us to use more renewable energy?

Think about all the things that you know about fossil fuels, nuclear energy, and renewable energy. Decide if the information is positive or negative. Use the table below to write your answers.

	Fossil Fuels	Nuclear Energy	Renewable Energy
Good			
Bad			

Warm-Up Questions

1. Do you think it is important that we have electricity?

2. Is it easy for people to use less energy?

3. Do you think energy should be free?

Renewable Energy

The number of people in the world is growing very quickly. In sixty years, about 11 billion people will live on Earth. All these people will need energy. Fossil fuels have helped us to develop our world. But we may need to use more renewable energy.

Some people argue that we should start using renewable energy. One reason is that fossil fuels have created a lot of pollution. This has caused our world to become hotter. A warmer world is a problem because many areas will be flooded. In other words, the areas will become covered with water. Another reason is that fossil fuels are running out. Some day, all the fossil fuels will be gone. This will be a serious problem if we do not have renewable energy.

Other people argue that we should not start using renewable energy. They say that we should continue to use fossil fuels. Renewable energy cannot supply all the energy we need. If we stop using fossil fuels, we will not have enough power to use our cellphones, computers, or cars. Everyone will be very unhappy. Another problem is that renewable energy is very expensive. Many countries cannot afford to produce this type of energy. Fossil fuels are much cheaper.

Comprehension Check

Answer the questions using information from the reading passage.

1. How many people will live on Earth in sixty years?

2. Why is it a problem that our world is becoming hotter?

3. Why should we develop renewable energy?

4. What will happen if we stop using fossil fuels?

5. Why can many countries not afford to produce renewable energy?

Vocabulary Check

Complete each sentence with one of the words below.

flooded	fossils	fuels	produced	supply

1. Climate change has _____ bad results.

2. This food will _____ your body with energy.

3. Last weekend, it rained so much that some of the city was _____.

4. Most _____ were made many thousands of years ago.

5. We burn _____ to create energy.

Opinion Practice

Practice supporting and refuting the opinions below.

Supporting Opinions

1. It is very important for Korea to develop and use renewable energy…

2. Many countries need to sell fossil fuels…

3. We have to keep using fossil fuels…

4. Using renewable energy will help to slow down climate change…

ⓐ because renewable energy is not available freely.

ⓑ because those are the only things the countries have to make money.

ⓒ because this kind of energy is very clean.

ⓓ because the country buys expensive fossil fuels from other countries.

Refuting Opinions

1. Nuclear energy is very clean.

2. Fossil fuels are much cheaper than renewable energy.

3. We are running out of fossil fuels.

4. We don't need fossil fuels. There are many different kinds of energy that we can use.

ⓐ I disagree. We cannot use other kinds of energy effectively. We need fossil fuels so that we can have enough energy.

ⓑ I disagree. When it goes wrong, nuclear energy will make the environment very dirty.

ⓒ I don't think so. Fossil fuels are more expensive than some types of renewable energy.

ⓓ I don't think so. Engineers are discovering large amounts of oil and gas all the time.

Opinion Examples

Read the opinions and answer the questions.

 Supporting Opinion

We must use more renewable energy. One reason is that it will benefit South Korea. The country does not have any fossil fuels. As a result, Korea needs to buy fossil fuels from other countries. This is expensive and unreliable. Another reason is that the world is running out of fossil fuels. Sometimes, scientists find some amounts of oil and gas, but these fossil fuels are very difficult to obtain. In addition, we may destroy the environment if we try to take the fuels out. Therefore, we should develop renewable energy.

 Opposing Opinion

We need to keep using fossil fuels to obtain enough energy. To begin with, renewable energy cannot produce enough power for everyone in the world. Scientists have been developing solar, wind, and water power for a long time. But these scientists have failed to help us have enough power. Second, fossil fuels are much cheaper. Renewable energy is too expensive. So, most people cannot afford to pay a lot of money for that type of energy. If we keep using fossil fuels and nuclear energy, citizens can save more money.

1. Circle the main idea in each opinion.

2. Underline the supporting ideas in each opinion.

3. Can you think of some examples to support the ideas in each opinion?

Discussion Questions

Discuss these questions in groups.

1. Do you think it is important for Korea to develop renewable energy?

2. South Korea has a lot of nuclear power plants. Should the country continue to use them?

3. Is it a problem that fossil fuels are polluting our Earth?

4. Why do you think many companies want to keep using fossil fuels?

5. Can we live without electricity?

Let's Debate

Choose one of the statements below and then debate in groups.

1. We should stop using fossil fuels and nuclear power.

2. Having enough energy is more important than the environment.

3. The price of energy should be much higher to stop people from wasting it.